To my parents, Ruth and Al—R. G.

To learn more about Rob Gonsalves's work, or to find his work in a gallery near you,
please visit www.discoverygalleries.com or the Discovery Gallery at 4840 Bethesda Avenue,
Bethesda, Maryland 20814; (301) 913-9199.

Atheneum Books for Young Readers
An imprint of Simon & Schuster Children's Publishing Division
1230 Avenue of the Americas
New York, New York 10020
Text copyright © 2008 by Sarah L. Thomson
Illustrations copyright © 2008 by Rob Gonsalves
All rights reserved, including the right of reproduction on whole or in part in any form.
Book design by Krista Vossen
The text of this book is set in Centaur and Oberon.
The illustrations for this book are rendered in acrylics.
Manufactured in the United States of America
1 2 3 4 5 6 7 8 9 10

First Edition
Library of Congress Cataloging-in-Publication Data
Thomson, Sarah L.
Imagine a place / Sarah L. Thomson ; illustrated by Rob Gonsalves.—1st ed.
p.   cm.
Summary: Illustrations and evocative text show how imagination can reveal the extraordinary
in the everyday.
ISBN-13: 978-1-4169-6802-3
ISBN-10: 1-4169-6802-4
[1. Imagination—Fiction.] I. Gonsalves, Rob, ill. II. Title.
PZ7.T378Imd 2008
[E]—dc22   2008007107

imagine

A PLACE

Imagi

Atheneum Books for Young Readers

NEW YORK   LONDON   TORONTO   SYDNEY

ne A PLACE

words by SARAH L. THOMSON

paintings by ROB GONSALVES

imagine a place . . .

. . . where you bend and sway,

    leap and land,

    right where a story

    begins.

imagine a place . . .

. . . where water is solid,

light is liquid,

sky a frozen river

flowing under your feet.

imagine a place . . .

. . . where your mind opens wider
than any walls around you.

imagine a place . . .

. . . where freedom is

as sweet as falling water,

light as a feather welcomed

into the gentle air.

imagine a place . . .

. . . where spring becomes

an avalanche of blossoms,

a torrent of sweetness

overflowing the earth.

imagine a place . . .

. . . where your ship holds

all you once knew

and the horizon offers

all you will ever need.

imagine a place . . .

. . . where time is counted

by ticks and tocks,

but space is measured

in sunset.

imagine a place . . .

. . . where each turn

takes you home.

imagine a place . . .

. . . where the tang of pine

meets the salt of sea,

where adventure finds

a waiting heart.

imagine a place . . .

. . . where words shelter you,

ideas uphold you, and

thoughts lead you

to the secret

inside the labyrinth.

imagine a place . . .

. . . where brick and mortar

dig deep roots,

where buds unfurl

as soft as sunlight,

strong as stone.

imagine a place . . .

. . . where fire is cool

against your skin,

a glimmering echo

of a star.

imagine a place . . .

. . . where music sings

in every breeze

of a summer night,

and the wind twirls you

in a waltz

that lasts until dawn.

imagine a place . . .

. . . where castle and cloud

shift from square to square

and the world lies

in the winner's hand.

imagine a place . . .

. . . where the sigh of surf

and the whisper of waves

spill from your suitcase

and drift into your dreams.

Imagine . . . here.